A Season at Glyndebourne

A Season at Glyndebourne

IRA NOWINSKI

Foreword by
Lord Gibson

CHRISTOPHER HELM
London

© 1988 Ira Nowinski
Christopher Helm (Publishers) Ltd, Imperial House,
21-25 North Street, Bromley, Kent BR1 1SD

ISBN 0-7470-2407-3

A CIP catalogue record for this book
is available from the British Library

Printed in Great Britain by Westerham Press Ltd, Westerham, Kent
Bound by Hunter and Foulis Ltd, Edinburgh

CONTENTS

FOREWORD

If I may be forgiven for beginning on a personal note, my earliest recollection of Glyndebourne is of a visit in June 1928. I was twelve years old and my parents, who both sang and were frequent visitors to Glyndebourne before the Festival was founded or the opera house built, were taking part in an amateur performance of the first scene of Act III of *Meistersinger*. It took place in the organ room and John Christie, our host, sang Beckmesser, my father Hans Sachs and my mother Eva.

Neighbours came to listen. A piano and the organ took the place of an orchestra. What I best remember about it is the pleasure the performance gave the performers. However, since in those days standards of recorded music were not high and opportunities of hearing professional musicians were less frequent than today, perhaps it pleased the audience too. Certainly its reception gave John Christie enough encouragement to plan further operatic events, and my mother suggested that he should invite Audrey Mildmay, a young singer then at the beginning of her career whom John had not yet met, to sing at Glyndebourne. She agreed to do so. Not long afterwards she and John were married, a sequel for which Sir George Christie has expressed what he calls 'atavistic gratitude' to the Gibson family.

It was, of course, for Audrey that John built the opera house, which opened with *Figaro* in 1934, Audrey singing a delicious Susanna. I recall it as one of the most exciting occasions of my life. It was not only a unique experience to hear opera intended to reach the highest international standards in the theatre of a country house. Even more remarkable, such standards were attained and, in at least one respect surpassed, for it was a revelation of what could be accomplished, in both production and ensemble, when first-class musicians were brought together and enabled to rehearse for many weeks without distraction.

Thus, in the years leading up to the war John Christie realised his dream and set new levels of operatic accomplishment. Which of us, however, attending that first Glyndebourne season, could have believed that so eccentric an ambition, as it then seemed, as the presentation of first class opera among the Sussex Downs would not only be achieved, but continued into the second generation, and that Glyndebourne's 50th Anniversary would be passed with the Festival acclaimed by critics and public from all over the world. It is an extraordinary story. Since 1934 conditions for the performance of opera have changed no less than any other aspect of life, but what succeeded against all expectations in the thirties has, under George Christie's leadership, shone no less brilliantly in the last 28 years. The Festival has broadened its repertoire and adapted its policies in a changing world, consistently maintaining the highest standards in music, production and design.

Yet, in spite of the professionalism that has been a prerequisite of this success, Glyndebourne remains a family home and it is this background to the Festival that helps to enchant its visitors. In these photographs Ira Nowinski has captured the spirit of the place and all that happens there.

Lord Gibson
*Lord Gibson was a Trustee of the Glyndebourne Arts Trust
from 1968 to 1972 and from 1977 to 1986.*

INTRODUCTION

My invitation to Ira Nowinski to spend the summer of 1987 at Glyndebourne came as a result of a meeting in San Francisco in September 1986 when Ira showed me his recent work at the San Francisco Opera, in particular and most spectacularly the photographs he took of the famous San Francisco *Ring* Cycles of 1985. Remarkable too were the many informal shots of artists taken off-stage and those on-stage pictures taken from unusual angles which contribute so much to the 'Nowinski look'. Ira's enthusiasm for the idea of working at Glyndebourne fired mine for a new view of Glyndebourne through the lens of a man whose documentary work in non-operatic fields is in many of the most distinguished private and public photograph collections in the United States. My determination was reinforced on seeing his exhibition at the New York Public Library at Lincoln Center in November 1986.

I am grateful, in particular to George and Mary Christie for having taken Ira and his project to their hearts; and to the Glyndebourne Association America Inc. whose generous sponsorship made this unique Anglo-American enterprise possible.

Brian Dickie
General Administrator

THE THEATRE AND PHOTOGRAPHY

If Henry James spent his life in the search for *le mot juste* — the perfect word for each context that would crystallise, embody and illuminate — the theatre photographer searches for the photographic equivalent, *le moment juste*, which most perfectly captures drama, emotion, time and place.

For over 60 years after the invention of photography there is no particular genre that can be designated 'theatre photography'; from the millions of photographs actors can only be discerned by the more assured way in which they face the camera or by known costuming or grouping. Not until the beginning of the century were specialist photographers established, working in the studio and the theatre itself. Banks of extra floodlights had to be used, which emphasised the two-dimensional look of the set, but the aim was to record the look, not the experience of a production.

By the 1920s, although equipment was still cumbersome, it was possible to photograph from the auditorium during a performance using available stage light. Taken from a distance to minimise movement, these give for the first time an idea of what audiences actually saw. In the next decade the development of the miniature camera, together with faster films and lenses, gave greater mobility and flexibility, so that individual performances could be recorded from close to the stage or even from the wings.

For publicity and front-of-house pictures, however, managements relied upon the posed photocall. Significant scenes were recreated and specially lit for the camera, and a master such as Angus McBean could perfectly encapsulate the theatrical experience in photographs of great power and insight and the highest possible technical quality. It was glamour treatment for an age of great theatrical glamour.

By the 1950s the photocall had become an expensive luxury for many theatres. Such formal high definition photographs were, anyway, less expressive of a new realistic drama than the grainy, harsher images produced by the miniature camera. The photographer now became an invited guest at the dress rehearsal, and had to develop instinctive reflexes to recognise and capture the significant moment, and new technical skills to compensate for generally dimmer stage lighting.

Ira Nowinski's work turns back the clock to produce images that exploit the dynamic flexibility of the miniature camera, while matching the high technical quality of the plate camera and the posed photocall. His control of available light, whether natural, indoor or stage lighting, is extraordinary. Never mere illumination, it plays an almost tangible part, enveloping and enfolding landscape and people, forming and modelling, emphasising his fascination with texture and structure. Not for him the black hole to which players are condemned by the gloom of modern stage lighting. He sees people in relation to their surroundings, and uses stage sets, environment and landscape not only to create mood and atmosphere, but also to explain and enhance the figures, whether singers, orchestra, the Glyndebourne staff or the audience.

He photographs with an objective passion which is so much more than photo-journalism. Many have recorded the theatre at work and in performance, but few with his intimacy and involvement which stem from complete familiarity and understanding of the subject and the instinctive recognition of the *moment juste*. Eschewing the curse of the backstage photographer, the superficial that degenerates into the sentimental, Nowinski goes beneath the surface, beneath emotion and drama to a point where he becomes part of the experience, be it on stage or among the audience. Like a painter he chooses the significant viewpoint that gives maximum involvement, and as with few other photographers we become participants in, not vicarious voyeurs of, this private world of rehearsal and performance. Not surprisingly, the painter he most calls to mind is Degas — and it gives some idea of his reflexes and technical skill that in the split second he perceives structure and angles of vision which a painter constructs at leisure in the studio.

Through the camera he sees the world with a pinsharp clarity, so unlike normal focused vision that photographs take on the detailed clarity of a dream. This is reinforced by an extraordinarily highly developed compositional sense, which perceives formal structure and patterns amid the random chaos of normality. It is, indeed, sometimes difficult to believe that the photographs were not posed — the relation between singer and set, between foreground and background, the placing of a bench or a background figure, seem obvious because inevitable; the elusive moment is held in a severe, often geometric, composition that reflects the formality of the Glyndebourne landscape and the stage settings and gives to that transient second an almost universal significance. Yet in freezing time at this moment of maximum significance he does not create a dead image, but one in which is sensed past and future existence.

Opera being an inherently static art, its photographic appeal was always more limited than that of drama or dance. It retained the nineteenth-century star traditions well into the present century, and photographs like Nowinski's would have been impossible in an age when, irrespective of country or production, itinerant stars stood firmly centre stage and gave their own performance. Slowly a new breed of 'acting singers' using body and face as well as voice to express emotion, evolved and, in a few opera houses, notably Glyndebourne itself, they were developed as part of an integrated production — a trend that did not become general in opera until the post-war period. But even today photographs of opera singers are often characterised by the strain and exaggerated emotion that come from the physical effort of singing, or are mere production records. What Nowinski makes clear is something more subtly characteristic — the intensity of concentration in rehearsal and performance, demanded by listening not only to themselves, but themselves balanced against each other, against the chorus and against the orchestra — the total absorption in the mechanics and art of singing.

The artist, whatever his medium, opens our eyes to the unknown, but also confronts us with the shock of the familiar. We live in a world so prolific of images that there is a danger that all images are devalued, and we forget that there should be a quality beyond the superficial recording of 'reality'. The words 'theatre', 'opera', 'Glyndebourne' conjure up pictures in the mind — pictures that are themselves often second-hand and hackneyed. Nowinski's achievement is not to record and endorse those stereotypes but represent them with new force, so that we not only see them anew, but experience them for the first time.

Sarah C. Woodcock
Theatre Museum, London

ACKNOWLEDGEMENTS

I would like to thank George and Mary Christie for their hospitality and interest in my work; Brian Dickie for bringing me to Glyndebourne and helping me edit the photographs for publication; Helen O'Neill for her editorial direction and Joanna Townsend for co-ordinating the project on both sides of the Atlantic and smoothing out all the problems.

My thanks to Richard Bradshaw for introducing me to Brian Dickie and Glyndebourne; to Martin Isepp, Jean Mallandaine, Craig Rutenberg and all the music staff. Special thanks to Tom Redman, who encouraged me to return last Fall to photograph *The Electrification*, to Stage Management, the technical departments, the Chorus and Ivor Bolton; also to Janet Moores, who made my stay in Ringmer a wonderful experience, to John Harden and Adrian Wines.

I would especially like to thank all the artists for their encouragement and co-operation, allowing me to point my camera at them at the most unusual moments.

I am greatly indebted to the Glyndebourne Association America Inc. for the grant which made the whole project a reality, to E. Leitz Inc. of America and Wolfgang Baumann for the loan of equipment, and to John Parsons-Smith of Kodak for providing me with film and paper to make the prints for the book.

Finally, thanks to John Parfitt of Westerham Press, Production Manager Darina Williams, and to Christopher Helm for making it all possible.

Dedicated to Robin Endsley-Fenn.

Ira Nowinski
San Francisco, March 1988

A Season at
Glyndebourne

1. *Sir George Christie*

2. *Foxgloves in the gardens*

3. *The Urn garden*

4. *Jack Brymer, guest principal clarinet with the London Philharmonic Orchestra, posing in the gardens*

5. *Festival poster at the entrance*

6. *Lilies on the pond*

7. *Choosing a picnic spot*

8. *Front of the Christies' house*

9. *View across the gardens from the croquet lawn*

10. *Mary Christie celebrates her birthday with her husband George*

11. *Before the performance*

12. *A stroll by the pond*

13. *A view of the opera house*

14. *Artistic Director, Sir Peter Hall, and Musical Director, Bernard Haitink before the first night of* Carmen

LA TRAVIATA

15. *Marie McLaughlin in the Green Room before a performance*

16. *Masked chorister before Flora's party*

17. *Brent Ellis and Marie McLaughlin*

18. *Backstage view of Flora's party*

19. *Flora's party*

20. *Child dancers: Teresa Hinde, Kelly Earl, Isabel Mant*

21. *Act II, scene ii: Jane Turner as Flora*

22. *Peter Hall in rehearsal with Marie McLaughlin*

23. *Final dress rehearsal: Marie McLaughlin and Walter MacNeil*

24.   *Chorus warm-up in the Green Room*

25. *First night curtain call: Bernard Haitink*

CARMEN

26. *Barry McCauley*

27. *Conductor Graeme Jenkins during a music rehearsal in the Organ Room*

28. *Maria Ewing in the Green Room before a performance*

29. *Maria Ewing during a quick costume change in the wings*

30. *French coach Marguerite Meyerowitz with Faith Esham in her dressing room before a performance*

31. *Chorus Master, Ivor Bolton conducts off-stage during Act IV*

32. *Carmen faces the shadow of Don José*

33. *Final scene*

34. *Dressing room corridor after fight scene in Act III. David Holloway and Barry McCauley*

35. *Louise Winter*

36. *Curtain call with Mariana Cioromila as Carmen*

Così fan tutte

37. Music rehearsal in the Organ Room: Gabriele Fontana and Frank Lopardo

MOZART,
Born 1756.—Died 1791.
Pompeo Battoni Rome 1779.

38. *Portrait of Mozart in the Organ Room*

39. *Dale Duesing*

40. *Isobel Buchanan at a costume fitting with Chief Cutter, Jean Hunnisett*

41. *Production rehearsal: Isobel Buchanan, Dale Duesing, Gabriele Fontana and Frank Lopardo*

42. *Frank Lopardo*

43. *Frank Lopardo, Isobel Buchanan, Claudio Desderi, Gabriele Fontana, Dale Duesing*

44. *End of Act I seen from the General Administrator's box*

45. *Commedia dell' arte figure*

CAPRICCIO

46. *Bernard Haitink*

47. *Martin Isepp, Head of Music Staff, in the Organ Room*

48. *Music rehearsal: Felicity Lott and Anne Howells*

49. *Alastair Miles, Colin McKerracher, Howard Milner with Director John Cox*

50. *Dancers at rehearsal: Ian Knowles and Carol Grant*

51. Production rehearsal: Olaf Bär and John Cox

52. *Orchestral rehearsal: Graeme Jenkins and Bernard Haitink in the pit*

53. *Octogenarian Hugues Cuenod prepares for a performance*

54. *A scene taken from the wings*

55. *Olaf Bär as the Count poses outside the theatre*

56. *Felicity Lott and Hugues Cuenod play to the camera in the wings*

L'HEURE ESPAGNOLE

L'Enfant et les Sortilèges

57. Simon Rattle

58. *Louise Winter, Lillian Watson and Fiona Kimm*

59. *Maurice Sendak painting Maurice Ravel*

60. *Thierry Dran*

61. *Production rehearsal of* L'heure espagnole : *Director Frank Corsaro with Anna Steiger*

62. *Stage rehearsal: Thierry Dran, François Loup and Frank Corsaro*

63. *François Loup*

64. *Lillian Watson as the Nightingale*

65. *Ballet rehearsal, Paulo Lopes and Colleen Barsley*

66. *Backstage warm-up*

67. *Fiona Kimm as The Cat*

68. *Anna Steiger backstage with Stage Manager,*
    Lucy Stewart-Roberts, waiting to take her curtain call while Rémy
    Corazza acknowledges applause

Porgy and Bess

69. *Music rehearsal: Willard White and Cynthia Haymon*

70. *Cynthia Haymon*

71. *Conductor Richard Bradshaw*

72. *Trevor Nunn with Associate Director, Alby James*

73. *Trevor Nunn giving notes during production rehearsal*

74. *Rehearsal for the crap game*

75. *Willard White*

76. *Gregg Baker after on-stage fight*

77. Marietta Simpson

78. *Robins's funeral: Cynthia Haymon as Bess*

79. 'There's a boat dat's leavin' soon for New York . . .' Cynthia Haymon and Damon Evans

80. *'Bess you is my woman now, . . .' Cynthia Haymon and Willard White*

81. 'Bess, oh where's my Bess, . . .' Willard White

82. *General Administrator Brian Dickie*

83. *The hurricane scene: Gregg Baker and Marietta Simpson*

THE ELECTRIFICATION OF THE SOVIET UNION

Glyndebourne Touring Opera

The London Sinfonietta Opera Orchestra

World Premiere, 5 October 1987

84. *Omar Ebrahim as the poet Serezha*

85. The creative team: Craig Raine, Peter Sellars, Nigel Osborne, James F. Ingalls

86. *Pasternak with his younger alter-ego Serezha, Henry Herford and Omar Ebrahim*

87. Linda Hirst

88. *Omar Ebrahim and Elizabeth Laurence*

89. *Eirian Davies*

90. *In rehearsal: Elizabeth Laurence and Omar Ebrahim*

91. *'You mustn't force your inspiration.*
    Just take your time.'
    Omar Ebrahim and Philip O'Reilly

92. *The nameless of the human race
will stand together and alone,
without a heart, without a face,
till thrones are overthrown.'
Omar Ebrahim and Henry Herford*

93. *'You were a gentle boy . . .'*
    Elizabeth Laurence and Omar Ebrahim

The Audience

95. *The strawberry eater*

96. *House Manager Geoffrey Gilbertson*

97. Interval dinner

98. *Champagne under the lime trees*

99. *Family portrait*

100.

101. *Interval croquet match: members of the London Philharmonic Orchestra*

102. *Robin in the garden*

104. *English music lovers*

105. *Mélomanes français*

111. Terence Parker, Head Gardener

113.

114. *George Christie with Phoebe*

NOTES BY IRA NOWINSKI

Equipment

For these photographs I used two Leicas — an M4 and an M6. The lenses used were an f2.8 Elmarit and two Sumicrons, a 35mm and 90mm. I also used a Nikon N2000 with 105mm f2.5 Nikkor. A Leitz tripod was used with the Nikon, and occasionally I used a monopod with the Leica, but usually used the Leica hand held. Prints were made with a Leitz Focomat 1-C with a 50mm Nikkor.

Exposure and lighting

I used Kodak film — T-Max 400, which has a sharper resolution and less grain than other black-and-white films. I always overexposed by at least a ½ stop and used no special lighting for either interiors or exteriors. The photographs are carefully composed by a geometric balance of available light and subject with texture and detail.

The exposures were determined by careful examination of developed negatives and after the first test films I was able to calculate the various exposures without the use of a meter. The film was developed in a T-Max developer, diluted 1:4 at 72°F, in a four-reel stainless steel tank. Development time was 6½ minutes, followed by a 30-second water bath, and then a rapid fix for 10 minutes. This film has an extra thick emulsion which requires a longer fixing time. I used Photo-Flow before hanging the negatives to dry.

I exposed 340 rolls of T-Max film throughout this project and developed the negatives in my apartment in Ringmer. This enabled me to comprehend fully the scope of the work, and by careful monitoring I was able to keep the opacity at a constant level.

Prints

To produce the publication and exhibition prints, I used Kodak Elite Paper, grades 2 and 3. This paper has a long tonal range and a hard emulsion coated with plenty of silver. This allows for long development times and contrast control. The paper also responds well to selenium toner, which gives the prints added shadow and detail and makes them suitable for archival preservation.

A split development technique was used with Kodak Selectol-Soft and Dektol developers. The prints were first put into a 68°F solution of Selectol-Soft diluted 1:1 for 1 minute and then transferred to Dektol, diluted 1:2. This split development allowed control of highlights and enhancement of detail. Dektol strengthens the blacks and gives the shadow area a good contrast.

After the prints developed a full tonal range (sometimes 4 minutes in the developer) they were transferred to a stop-bath solution and then to a fixing bath for 10 minutes. After thorough washing the prints were transferred to a second fixing bath prepared without hardener, thence to a selenium toning bath containing Hypo-Clear for 2 minutes under a strong light.

After washing the prints they were put on drying racks for 24 hours, followed by a 1 minute pressing at 270°F. The prints were then retouched with a fine type 0 brush using spot tone retouching agent.

Ira Nowinski
San Francisco
March 1988

CREDITS

Glyndebourne

Festival Opera

Founded in 1934 by Audrey and John Christie
General Administrator: Brian Dickie
Musical Director: Bernard Haitink, KBE   *Artistic Director:* Sir Peter Hall, CBE

LA TRAVIATA

Opera in three Acts
Music by Guiseppe Verdi
Libretto by Francesco Maria Piave

In the original Italian

Conductors	BERNARD HAITINK
	SIAN EDWARDS *from 29 June*
Director	PETER HALL
Associate Director	CHRISTOPHER NEWELL
Designer	JOHN GUNTER
Lighting Designer	DAVID HERSEY
Choreographer	ELIZABETH KEEN

CAST

Violetta Valéry, *a courtesan*	MARIE McLAUGHLIN
Flora Bervoix, *a friend*	JANE TURNER
Marchese d'Obigny	CHRISTOPHER THORNTON-HOLMES
Baron Douphol, *a rival of Alfredo*	GORDON SANDISON
Doctor Grenvil	JOHN HALL
Gastone, Viscount de Letorières	DAVID HILLMAN
Alfredo Germont, *Violetta's lover*	WALTER MacNEIL
Annina, *Violetta's maid*	ENID HARTLE
Giuseppe, *Violetta's servant*	MARTYN HARRISON
Giorgio Germont, *Alfredo's father*	BRENT ELLIS
Messenger	CHARLES KERRY

Performances on May 24, 27, 30, June 1, 4, 7, 11, 14, 17, 20, 23, 26, 29, July 2, 5
New production sponsored by B.A.T Industries

CARMEN

Opera in four Acts, based on the novel by Prosper Mérimée
Music by Georges Bizet
Libretto by Henri Meilhac and Ludovic Halévy

In the original French

Conductor	GRAEME JENKINS
Original Director	PETER HALL
Revival Director	AIDAN LANG
Design and Lighting	JOHN BURY
Choreographer	ELIZABETH KEEN

CAST

Moralès, *an officer*	PETER COLEMAN-WRIGHT
Micaëla, *a peasant girl*	FAITH ESHAM
Don José, *a corporal of dragoons*	BARRY McCAULEY
Zuniga, *a captain*	XAVIER DEPRAZ
Carmen, *a gypsy*	MARIA EWING
	*MARIANA CIOROMILA
Frasquita ⎫ *gypsies, friends of Carmen*	ANNA STEIGER
Mercédes ⎭	LOUISE WINTER
Lillas Pastia	OLIVIER PIERRE
Escamillo, *a toreador*	DAVID HOLLOWAY
Le Dancaïre ⎫ *smugglers*	GORDON SANDISON
Le Remendado ⎭	PETROS EVANGELIDES
Guide	FRÉDÉRIC ROSTAND

Performances on May 26, 29*, 31, June 2*, 6, 9, 13, 15, 18*, 21*, 25*, 28*
Production sponsored in 1985 by Citicorp Investment Bank Limited

126

COSI FAN TUTTE

ossia La scuola degli amanti

Comic opera in two Acts
Music by Wolfgang Amadeus Mozart
Libretto by Lorenzo da Ponte

In the original Italian

Conductor LOTHAR ZAGROSEK
Director PETER HALL
Associate Director STEPHEN LAWLESS
Design and Original Lighting JOHN BURY
Lighting revived by MARK JONATHAN

CAST

Ferrando FRANK LOPARDO
Guglielmo DALE DUESING
Don Alfonso CLAUDIO DESDERI
Fiordiligi GABRIELE FONTANA
Dorabella ISOBEL BUCHANAN
Despina LILLIAN WATSON
Harpsichord continuo played by MARTIN ISEPP
JEAN MALLANDAINE *from 10 July*

Performances on June 12, 16, 19, 24, 27, 30, July 4, 10, 12, 16, 19, 24, August 1, 4
Production sponsored in 1978 by National Westminster Bank

CAPRICCIO

A musical conversation piece
Music by Richard Strauss
Text by Clemens Krauss and Richard Strauss
Published by Boosey and Hawkes Music Publishers Ltd

In the original German

Conductors BERNARD HAITINK
GRAEME JENKINS *from 26 July*
Director JOHN COX
Assistant Director DAVID EDWARDS
Designers DENNIS LENNON *(Scenery)*
MARTIN BATTERSBY *(Costumes and furniture)*
Lighting Designer ROBERT BRYAN
Original Choreography PAULINE GRANT
Revived by JENNY WESTON

CAST

Flamand, *a composer* DAVID KUEBLER
Olivier, *a poet* PETER WEBER
La Roche ERNST GUTSTEIN
The Countess FELICITY LOTT
The Count, *her brother* OLAF BÄR
Clairon, *an actress* ANNE HOWELLS
An Italian Tenor JEAN-LUC VIALA
An Italian Soprano FIORELLA PEDICONI
Major-Domo GEOFFREY MOSES
Monsieur Taupe, *a prompter* HUGUES CUENOD
Servants PATRICK DONNELLY, COLIN McKERRACHER,
ALASTAIR MILES, HOWARD MILNER, DAVID OWEN,
ROBERT POULTON, GERARD QUINN, CHRISTOPHER VENTRIS
Dancers CAROL GRANT, IAN KNOWLES
Harpsichord played by IAIN LEDINGHAM
JONATHAN HINDEN *from 21 July*

Performances on July 6, 9, 11, 13, 15, 18, 21, 23, 26, August 2, 5, 9
Revival sponsored by Imperial Chemical Industries PLC

L'HEURE ESPAGNOLE

Comic opera in one Act
Music by Maurice Ravel
Libretto by Franc-Nohain

L'ENFANT ET LES SORTILEGES

Lyric fantasy in two parts
Music by Maurice Ravel
Libretto by Colette

By permission of Editions Arima Ltd and Editions Durand SA Paris/UMP

In the original French

Conductors SIMON RATTLE
SIAN EDWARDS *21 August*
Director FRANK CORSARO
Associate Director STEPHEN LAWLESS
Designer MAURICE SENDAK
Lighting Designer ROBERT ORNBO
Film Animator & Slide Designer RONALD CHASE
Choreographer JENNY WESTON

CASTS

L'HEURE ESPAGNOLE

Ramiro, *a muleteer* FRANÇOIS LE ROUX
Torquemada, *a clockmaker* RÉMY CORAZZA
Concepcion, *wife of Torquemada* ANNA STEIGER
Gonzalve, *a poet* THIERRY DRAN
Don Inigo Gomez, *a banker* FRANÇOIS LOUP

L'ENFANT ET LES SORTILEGES

The Child CYNTHIA BUCHAN
His Mother FIONA KIMM
The Tom Cat MALCOLM WALKER
The Armchair FRANÇOIS LOUP
The Louis XV Chair HYACINTH NICHOLLS
The Grandfather Clock MALCOLM WALKER
The Tea Pot THIERRY DRAN
The Chinese Cup LOUISE WINTER
The Fire LILLIAN WATSON
A Shepherd JADY PEARL
A Shepherdess CAROL SMITH
The Princess HAROLYN BLACKWELL
The Little Old Man (Arithmetic) THIERRY DRAN
The Cat FIONA KIMM
A Tree FRANÇOIS LOUP
The Dragonfly LOUISE WINTER
The Nightingale LILLIAN WATSON
The Bat HYACINTH NICHOLLS
The Squirrel ANNA STEIGER
The Frog THIERRY DRAN
The Little Owl ALISON HAGLEY
Bat/Louis XV Chair LYNNE DAVIES
Dancers PAULO LOPES, COLLEEN BARSLEY, NIGEL NICHOLSON

Performances on July 22, 25, 29, 30, August 7, 10, 11, 13, 15, 17, 19, 21
New production sponsored by IBM United Kingdom Trust

PORGY AND BESS

Music by GEORGE GERSHWIN
Lyrics by DuBOSE HEYWARD and IRA GERSHWIN
Libretto by DuBOSE HEYWARD
Based on the play *Porgy* by DOROTHY and DuBOSE HEYWARD
Presented by arrangement with
Tams-Witmark Music Library Inc, New York

Conductor	RICHARD BRADSHAW
Director	TREVOR NUNN
Associate Director	ALBY JAMES
Designers	JOHN GUNTER *(Sets)*
	SUE BLANE *(Costumes)*
Lighting Designer	DAVID HERSEY
Choreographer	CHARLES AUGINS
Fights arranged by	TERRY KING

CAST

Jasbo Brown, *a pianist*	WAYNE MARSHALL
Clara, *Jake's wife*	SHERYL MELVIN
Mingo	BARRINGTON COLEMAN
Sportin' Life	DAMON EVANS
Jake	BRUCE HUBBARD
Serena, *Robbins' wife*	CYNTHIA CLAREY
Robbins	RICHIE PITTS
Jim	CURTIS WATSON
Peter, *the honeyman*	MERVIN WALLACE
Lily, *Peter's wife*	MAUREEN BRATHWAITE
Maria	MARIETTA SIMPSON
Porgy	WILLARD WHITE
Crown	GREGG BAKER
Bess	CYNTHIA HAYMON
Undertaker	AUTRIS PAIGE
Annie	PAULA INGRAM
Frazier	WILLIAM JOHNSON
Scipio	NANA ANTWI-NYANIN
Nelson/Crab Man	COLENTON FREEMAN
Strawberry woman	CAMELLIA JOHNSON
Detective ALAN TILVERN	Coroner BILLY J. MITCHELL
Mr Archdale TED MAYNARD	Policeman RON TRAVIS

Performances on August 6, 8, 12, 14, 16, 18, 20, 22
Production sponsored in 1986 by Citicorp Investment Bank Limited

The London Philharmonic Orchestra
The Glyndebourne Chorus

THE ELECTRIFICATION OF THE SOVIET UNION

A new opera in two acts by NIGEL OSBORNE
Words by Craig Raine
Based on the novella *The Last Summer* by Boris Pasternak,
and on his poem *Spectorsky*

By permission of Universal Edition (London) Ltd

Sung in English

Conductor	ELGAR HOWARTH
Director	PETER SELLARS
Set Designer	GEORGE TSYPIN
Costume Designer	DUNÁ RAMICOVÁ
Lighting Designer	JAMES F INGALLS
Sound Projection	JOHN WHITING

CAST

Boris Pasternak	HENRY HERFORD
Serezha Spectorsky	OMAR EBRAHIM
Lemokh	JONATHAN VEIRA
Frestln/Sashka's husband	PHILIP O'REILLY
Fardybassov/Ticket Collector/	
Frestln Servant	WOUT OOSTERKAMP
Anna Arild	ELIZABETH LAURENCE
	SUSAN BICKLEY *(21 November)*
Sashka	ANNA STEIGER
Mrs Frestln	EIRIAN DAVIES
Natasha	LINDA HIRST
Harry Frestln	JAMIE GATES

Performances at Glyndebourne on October 5 (world premiere), 7, 24,
Oxford October 31, Southampton November 7, Manchester November 14,
Birmingham November 21

Commissioned for Glyndebourne by the BBC
Production sponsored by VINCENT MEYER